life
in the sea

Translation: Jean Grasso Fitzpatrick

All inquiries should be addressed to:
Barron's Educational Series, Inc.
250 Wireless Boulevard
Hauppauge, New York 11788

Library of Congress Catalog Card No. 87-12561

International Standard Book No. 0-8120-3865-7

Library of Congress Cataloging-in-Publication Data
Rius, María.
  Life in the sea.

  (Habitats)
  Translation of: La vida en el mar.
  Summary: Little Salmon observes a variety of living
things as he swims with Great Salmon down the river to the
sea. Includes factual information about animals that
live underwater.
  [1. Salmon — Fiction. 2. Marine animals — Fiction]
I. Parramón, José María. II. Title. III. Series: Rius,
María. Habitats.
PZ7.R5213Lj   1987   [E]   87-12561
ISBN 0-8120-3865-7

Printed in Spain

56   9960 987

habitats

life
in the sea

María Rius
J. M. Parramón

BARRON'S

Once upon a time there was a tiny fish named Salmon who lived in the waters of a river.

Salmon was very happy. He had a big family and lots of friends – especially the perch and the trout.

Time went by, and when Salmon was three years old, his teacher the Great Salmon told him, "Tomorrow we're going down the river to the sea."

The next day, they began their long trip down the river. Salmon was swimming alongside Great Salmon when all of a sudden he saw something that looked like a colorful little fish floating in the river. He was about to eat it up when Great Salmon called out, "Be careful!"

And then Great Salmon told all the fish that that was a hook. And behind a hook there was always a fisherman trying to catch trout and salmon.

They continued downstream. The river grew and grew wider and deeper, and there was more and more water to swim in until finally they reached the sea. And the sea was enormous and very deep!

And there were fish in the sea – big and small, in all different shapes and colors.

Salmon was very happy. He stuck his head up out of the water and saw a boat with lights on it. Some men in the boat were throwing ropes out to sea. "Let's get out of here!" shouted Great Salmon. "Those are fishermen throwing out their nets to catch us!"

Salmon and his leader quickly swam to the bottom of the sea. There Salmon saw a huge fish. "Stay away from him," Great Salmon shouted again. "Big fish eat small fish!"

The bottom of the sea was a wonderful place. They swam by a giant octopus, passed by a few seahorses, and watched a whale playing with a swordfish.

They swam toward the shore. Near the rocks they saw conches and crabs, shellfish and lobsters.

Down below, on the rocks and on the bottom of the sea, they saw all sorts of plants, sponges, and coral.

It was a fascinating world, with strange looking fish, seahorses and starfish, red and green plants.....It was all so exciting! IT WAS LIFE IN THE SEA!

LIFE IN THE SEA

The beauty of the sea is always changing, with many different kinds of fish and animal life, and a variety of plants and coral.

Life in the water

Many different kinds of plants and animals live underwater. This isn't too surprising when you consider that three-fourths of the earth's surface is covered by water. There are fish, amphibians, and shellfish underwater. Some birds can swim, too — the duck and the swan, for instance — and there are even mammals like the whale and the dolphin that live in the water.

Fish

Fish are vertebrates, which means they have a skeleton. They are born from eggs and are covered with scales. They use their fins to swim through the water. They may live in freshwater or salt water. Some fish, like the salmon, can live in either place.

Salmon

The red salmon is highly prized as food. It goes upriver to the stream where it was born to lay its eggs. It never gets lost on this journey, which makes biologists and zoologists believe that, like some birds, the salmon can guide itself by the stars or may have a special ability to find its way by sensing the temperature, smell, and other characteristics of the water. Not much is known about what salmon do in the ocean, except that they feed on plankton, which gives their flesh its distinctive pinkness.

Amphibians

Imagine you're near a lake. You're sure to hear a frog croaking. Frogs, like salamanders and certain other animals, live both in the water and on land. They're called *amphibians*. Throughout life, they change radically in appearance. Take frogs, for example: They begin as eggs. As babies, they live entirely in the water as legless tadpoles. Finally, they become frogs. This process is called *metamorphosis*.

Shellfish

Most shellfish live in the water. They are invertebrates, with no backbone. Their bodies may be protected by an outer shell, for example, snails, clams, and mussels. Sometimes the shell is part of their body, like the squid. Shellfish are very much appreciated for their delicate taste.